GUIDEBOOK TO MOBILE MASSAGE

TIPS FROM THE MASSAGE NINJA

Joann Brito

Joann Brito

COPYRIGHT & DISCLAIMER

COPYRIGHT

Copyright © 2018 by Joann Brito.
All rights reserved. This book or any portion thereof may not be reproduced or used in any manner whatsoever without the express written permission of the publisher except for the use of brief quotations in a book review.

Printed in the United States of America

ISBN 978-1-7327684-0-6

BODY BRITOPIA LLC
PO Box 550407
Houston, TX 77255
www.bodybritopia.com

COVER DESIGN

AMPLI Creative – www.amplicreative.com

DISCLAIMER

I am a Licensed Massage Therapist (LMT), Continuing Education Provider, and Massage Therapy Instructor in the State of Texas and NOT a Medical Doctor (MD). I do not diagnose any medical condition, nor prescribe any medications. Content in this book and website is for reference purposes only and is not a substitute for advice from a licensed health-care professional. You should not rely solely on this content, and Joann Brito and subsidiaries assumes no liability for inaccuracies.

Guidebook to Mobile Massage

Should you or a client need immediate medical or psychiatric assistance, please call 911 or seek immediate treatment at the nearest emergency room or hospital. Nothing listed within this book should be considered as medical advice for dealing with a given issue or problem. You should consult your health care professional for guidance for specific health problems.

This book is designed to be educational, instructive and informative in nature. I encourage you to make your own health care and business decisions based upon your own research, observations, experience and personal knowledge. The use of this information, recommendations, suggestions on services or products should be based on your own due diligence, and agree I am not liable for your success or failure in any aspect of your business. In addition, no individual, company or entity has paid me for said suggestions or recommendations on any services or products mentioned, and solely are my opinion and personal experience.

Table of Contents

COPYRIGHT & DISCLAIMER	2
AKNOWLEDGEMENTS	7
PRELUDE TO THE MASSAGE GAME	8
THE BASICS	10
License & Insurance	10
Company Structure & Branding	12
Navigation Software	13
Accessories	15
SUPPLIES	17
Massage Table & Chair	17
Sheets	19
Massage Carry Case	21
Music	23
Massage Lubricant	24
Mileage Tracker	26
COMMUNICATION	28
Safety	28
Phone	31
Email	32
Scheduling Software	33
Website	34
Listen and Adjust	36
Be Structured, But Flexible...	42

ACCEPTING PAYMENTS & PRICING   47

Establishing Pay Rate and Tips when
    traveling for a client   49
    Receipt and Invoices   59

MARKETING   61
    Explore & Find Your Niche Market
        61
- Business Cards   62
- Promotional Items   62
- Social Media   63
- Hotel & Highrises   67
- Networking 101   68
- Chair Massage Events   71
- Backstage Massage   80
- House calls   85
- Entertainment Venue   86
- Diversify How You Make Money   87

PRESENTATION IS KEY   89
- Punctuality   89
- Look   91
- Smell   92
- Nail Maintenance   93

MASSAGE ESSENTIALS BAG   96
TIPS ON WASHING LINEN   103
MODALITY OPTIONS   106

HOW TO HANDLE...   112
- Sexual Advances   113
- Unintentional Arousal   117

Cancellations	118
Domestics	119
Opposing Views	125
Confidentiality and Discretion	126

SELF-CARE	128
INVEST IN YOUR CRAFT	132
Never Stop Learning	132
Practice, Practice, Practice	133

PASSION	137
NOTES	140

FAVORITE QUOTES

Deepak Chopra	16
Warren Buffett	27
Bruce Lee	42
Eric Thomas	46
Gary Vaynerchuk	60
Oprah Winfrey	95
Michael Jordan	102
Tony Robbins	127
Eleanor Brown	131
TD Jakes	139

ACKNOWLEDGEDMENTS

To my daughter Sara, from the moment you entered this world you showed me the meaning of love. I'm honored & blessed to be your Mom.

Additionally, to my family, my friends and clients who have believed in me and my craft and contributed to my business throughout the years in efforts to see me grow and be successful.

THANK YOU!

PRELUDE TO THE MASSAGE GAME

Prior to massage, I owned a physical therapy and chiropractic clinic for several years primarily focusing on personal injury and workers compensation clients. We handled the rehab and recovery of individuals following a motor vehicle accident or injury on the job. I also coupled traditional rehab protocols with aquatic therapy, and installed a pool in my facility, as aquatics was my favorite therapeutic exercise to incorporate in the rehabilitation process. The water allowed for an effective form of therapy at any phase in the rehab process, which is why I enjoyed it so much.

It was my first real understanding of how the body responded to treatment, and the results and joy from client's, some who still are my friends to this day, intrigued me while giving me a great sense of fulfillment. So, once I chose to walk away from that field and begin my journey into my massage therapy career, I was inquisitive on all information regarding massage.

Throughout this book, my goal is to give you tips and recommendations to avoid some hiccups I encountered along the way, while also giving you the tools to help build your mobile massage practice. If you choose to have a massage space, many of these tips will still be useful for that massage model and you can simply adjust some of the suggestions to fit your scenario. A lot of this information I wish was available when I first entered the business, but I do hope all my experience and knowledge over the years brings you a lot of success in your business endeavors.

THE BASICS

Choosing to become a mobile massage therapist has many advantages and disadvantages. A major advantage is reducing the overhead expenses one may have with renting a massage space. Also, the ability to bring your massage practice virtually anywhere like homes, business', to parties and hotels, mixes up your office environment daily.

LICENSE & INSURANCE

Make sure your foundational structure of your business is in order before embarking on your mobile massage business. At the top of the list... you must have a valid massage therapy license that meets your state's required guidelines and your CEU hours must be current.

Carry your small replacement license with you in the event someone asks to see your license. This has only happened twice in my career, but once I showed my license information, I also sent the link to the state website so they could do a license verification on their own as well. It's useful for that client in the event they want to verify anyone else's license in the future. Save the therapist verification link under your state license information for quick reference.

Obtain Liability Massage Insurance – This may not be a requirement in some states, but it's a good investment, especially when starting out to protect yourself in the event any claims are brought against you. A few liability insurance options:

ABMP.com offers excellent coverage at either $199 or $229 for the year

AMTAmassage.org offers monthly insurance payment at $20 or $235 for the year

InsureBodywork.com offers a more cost-effective option at $96/year

> ▶ *Please refer to company websites to check current liability insurance rates for each company, as they could have changed.*

Vehicle Liability Insurance & Maintenance - Since constant driving is involved, make sure your car is in good working condition, and meets the minimum state requirements for liability coverage.

COMPANY STRUCTURE & BRANDING

Create a name for your business, and setup a *DBA or LLC*. When choosing a name, do a google and social media search first and see what all comes up when you type it in. The name of your business should be unique and depending on how your brand grows, you may want to trademark it in the future and take it to another level.

If the name you desire is used often or if you do a trademark search and find one similar in the same field, the trademark could be denied. You also won't create a strong web presence if you are competing with other companies with a similar name as yours.

Tax Planning - Consult with a tax attorney, CPA or accountant to plan how you will file your taxes and how to maintain proper records throughout the year.

Logo - Get with a graphic designer that can create a logo, so you can begin building your visual brand for your business.

Setup your system for client intake and medical history:

▶ Have a client intake form for the initial session with general client information, background/medical information, a liability release, have client sign the form and update it at least once a year.

▶ In the "notes" section of a client's contact in your phone, input important specific info, i.e. surgery and procedure dates, main problem areas, allergies, birthday/anniversary, and notate things they like/dislike during massage session for quick reference guide.

Also, since your phone is pivotal to managing your mobile massage business, it's highly advised to use a phone security option and make sure your phone locks. This way no one can pry into your important contact list and notes when you're not by your phone or in the event it's lost; which in turn protects your client's confidentiality.

NAVIGATION SOFTWARE

Getting to the location for your scheduled appointments, having the proper GPS to guide you and having the basic understanding of reading and operating your navigation system is vital to arriving to sessions on time. It also helps maintain and plan proper time management in between sessions.

Most vehicles have navigation installed, but if you want an additional option or do not have navigation in your car, here are a few more choices to choose from on your cellular device.

✗ Waze is a GPS app I use often because their platform is interactive. Other users will post police sightings, road hazards, wrecks, traffic delays, etc.

✗ Google Maps is another option as its been around for some time and very reliable.

To ensure the commute goes smoothly when going to a new location, I input the address in my phones navigation earlier that day and review the route it lays out. Also, it saves time since the address(s) are already input in the navigation, and you can simply click on it once you get into the vehicle and begin the commute. I also will add the address in my cars navigations because it's better to be overly prepared if one of the navigation devices loses signal or stops operating for some reason, so the other one can act as a backup. This has happened to me several times when going through patchy cell service areas.

Before using your cell phone as your GPS device, there are a few accessory suggestions to keep you safe and hands free from distraction.

ACCESSORIES

Bluetooth/AUX Connection - If your vehicle has a Bluetooth or even and Aux connection, pair it to your car or plug it in the aux port. There are also many Bluetooth aux devices on the market if you do not want to deal with any wires. You can also opt for a Bluetooth headset, but I would advise ear buds, and not full headphones that cover your entire ear, as you want to make sure you can hear and are alert for all the surroundings going on while driving.

Mount - Invest in a car mount to place your phone on so navigation is visible and your hands are free and on the steering wheel. Most states prohibit cell phone use while driving and if you're pulled over for violating this law, you're looking to pay a pretty penny for that ticket. If convicted, fines can range between $100 - $500 plus court costs. So, no texting or holding your cell phone to talk on the phone while driving.

Clock – Time management is an important component to each session. Bring a small digital LED clock or wear a watch to monitor your time.

Keep in mind that if you wear a watch while performing a massage, be sure to wear one that has a completely rubber band with no metal clasps. You would not want to scratch or injure a client during a session.

"The highest levels of performance come to people who are centered, intuitive, creative, and reflective – people who know to see a problem as an opportunity."

Deepak Chopra

SUPPLIES

MASSAGE TABLE & CHAIR

To become a mobile therapist, the first thing you need is a massage table. A massage chair is not required initially but is highly recommended as a future purchase, so you can diversify your massage options. If you're working with a budget like I was in the beginning, buy an affordable, but sturdy massage table. A relatively cheap massage chair can be found online as well for under $125. I currently have an Oakworks massage table and Oakworks massage chair, but I didn't start out with these items. Start small and as your money grows, you can invest in better quality supplies.

At one point I was purchasing a massage table every 6 - 8 months, because due to the stretching and the weight of the clients I was working on, the wood would simply begin to weaken because the quality wasn't the best and traveling also lessoned the tables shelf life. So, to maintain the client's safety and to ensure the table didn't break during a session, I did this for a few years.

I felt that option was the cheaper route at the time, rather than dropping over $600 for the table and accessories I wanted to purchase. I finally saved and was weeks away from making my table purchase when my client and his wife bought the exact table I wanted as a birthday gift for me (with some added accessories), and their assistant had it all setup and out after I finished the session; an unexpected but great surprise (Thanks Rita, Wade and Gabbi). ☺

Just proof that patience during this process was the right thing to do, so don't force or put yourself out buying the top of the line items upfront when you can't afford it. The things you desire will become attainable, but don't force it.

Nowadays, there are so many cost-effective ways to invest in tables, more options than when I first started. You can buy an above average massage table for $125 - $199 online that will last you minimally a year or longer depending on what type of massage work you do.

Go to:

- eBay
- Amazon
- Craigslist
- Massage Schools

Social media outlets, like Instagram or Facebook are other options to inquire about anyone selling a table.

SHEETS

Everyone has a different preference when it comes to sheets from color to the types of sheets to buy. My advice is to have a set of sheets that has consistent color flow and linen style.

Don't have sheet sets that clearly don't go together in a session, unless you're mixing specific colors deliberately to brand your company. For example, one therapist I mentored opted to have a black fitted sheet, green flat sheet and black top blanket.

She had to go thru a different company to purchase the desired flat sheets, but if you see her table setup, you recognize it's a massage being performed by her... simply an example of a unique way to brand your business.

If you choose to use a top blanket, it may vary in linen style from the sheets. Like flannel, quilted, micro plush or fleece blankets, but you do not want one too thick. The colors white, grey or black are good staple colors to start out with for both sheets and/or additional blanket.

If the sheets look sloppy, or clearly no effort was put into its presentation, a client will question if they are fresh and clean, or worse, question your overall quality of service.

As your income increases, you can get a custom top blanket with your logo or name on it to add extra class. This is also good for marketing purposes if a client takes a photo of the table prior or during the session, as your company can get added visual exposure.

☼ Tip

I always keep 1 - 2 extra sets of sheets in my car in the event I get a last-minute booking. There have been times when going back home would take too much time, so I would go to the store and get a brand-new set of sheets to optimize my time. So, to create from adding that expense and time, always stay prepared and have extra sets of sheets readily available. I also call that the "money attracter" because I always expect to get those last-minute calls or texts. The only dilemma is if one has the energy to do that extra session or opt to book the appointment in your next available time slot… which is a good problem to have.

MASSAGE CARRY CASE

Table Cart - When I first started out, I used a massage trolley/cart. This is not a bad option if you don't have to go over many curbs or levels and are strictly totting the table from one location to another. The downside is when you enter a client's house and must lift or maneuver the cart and table over levels (i.e. front door in most cases), you don't want to damage any of your client's property if the table gets off balance and wants to topple over. I'm constantly on uneven ground, so this ultimately was not the best option for me.

Carry case with wheels - I prefer a massage bag that has built-in wheels, or what some people call skates on the bottom of the carry case. It's easier to quickly adjust or lift my table if I happen to go over a surface that's not level, and I like being able to pack everything I need in the case without the worry of it toppling over. This is my go-to option for my table transport.

Table Harness - There is an invention by Doc Dossman called MobiLOOP which is basically a backpack harness you put around your table to free up your hands. It's particularly good if you must carry your table up any stairs, which is why I purchased the product as I had a sudden influx of clients with stairs.

I've come to accept that going up and down stairs with my table I'll never master as a therapist, but I also do not like people handling my table either (I know I'm weird), so the MobiLOOP has been great for those situations for me. It's also a good option if you work on the beach or stadiums as the wheels and/or trolley are more difficult to use in those settings.

If you are traveling to another city with your table, it's a good choice as you can use the harness to pack your table on your back, and then have free hands to wheel your luggage.

☼ Tip

I use Extremity Mobilization Straps for stretching (they resemble seatbelts), but when I do travel with my massage table, I use them to strap my luggage to my massage carry case at baggage claim so I can roll everything out together and relatively with ease.

Everyone has different needs and wants, so whichever option works for you, go for it.

MUSIC

Pandora is the longest music subscription I've had, but within the past year I also signed up for a *Spotify* account. The investment for one or both is worth it, because when a commercial randomly interrupts throughout the session, it really does spoil the mood. Again, don't put yourself out paying for a subscription if you can't afford it, as I didn't pay for my Pandora at first, but I use them so much now, that I do not regret the purchase.

You can start out paying for one service, and then later get the other if you desire a variety, but if paying for a subscription is not in your budget, still setup an account as both offer a free service option. Better to have a music option, even with commercials, then not having anything at all. You can simply tell a client you have said music account but let them know ahead of time it isn't a paid account, so when a commercial is played, at least they won't be surprised.

When I go to a client's place for the first time, and they don't want to watch television, I ask what they would like to listen to. If they are unsure, I ask what their favorite song or artist is and go from there. Typically, I use Pandora since that's what I'm most comfortable with it, but Spotify is great once you have created playlists or want to play a specific song or repeat a certain one. I use both accounts regularly for business and personal use during my commutes.

Most Commonly Used Pandora Stations:

✕ Calm Meditation Radio (spa music)

✕ Ocean Waves and Relaxing Music Radio (spa music)

✕ Floetry Radio (Soul & R&B)

Spotify: I have created custom playlists, and once those have played out, it will transition to the radio format.

☼ Tip

You can also use a client's tv cable music network to play music during a massage session.

MASSAGE LUBRICANT

Standard massage lubricant choices to use on the body:

° Oil   ° Lotion   ° Cream   ° Gel

When I initially started in the business, I used traditional massage creams and would alternate between that and oil. Today I still favor oil and cream, but I prefer the Shea Moisture brand because traditional massage brands and products would dry out my arms and hands since I washed them so much. I love the scents from the Shea Moisture brand, and it's a great base when I want to add and make my own concoction.

Ultimately, I choose products I like on my skin, but also pay attention to what your client's needs and preferences are. If you have someone that suffers from eczema then you would want to go with a lubricant like coconut oil or raw shea butter, to act as an extra moisturizer to smooth and soften skin and not cause it to flare up during the massage. Or for example, I have a client that does not like oil-based lubricants used on them for massage at all, so I'll have her choose which cream or lotion she prefers for the session.

I usually always have more than one massage lubricant type on hand in case a client doesn't like or may be sensitive to a product. This is another reason why I like the Shea Moisture brand because it's good for all skin types, and its one you don't mind keeping on after the session has ended.

Even when I go to get a massage, I take my own oil to the session because with some traditional massage lubricants, I feel like I HAVE to shower after because I do not like the overall feel or smell of what was used. So that's what got me to thinking, if I feel like this, so must my clients. I observed a difference when I switched to this brand and to this day, I will get asked by clients, "what is the oil or lotion that you used," and when I tell them, most go out and buy it.

With whatever brand you choose, remember that you are the main person using this product for several hours a day, so if you enjoy the overall smell and feel of it, then 90% of the time, your client will enjoy it as well.

MILEAGE TRACKER

If you want or plan on claiming a tax deduction for your mileage on your tax return, you will need a system in place to track all work mileage incurred for your tax return. When I tracked my mileage years ago, I kept a black journal in my car and had to manually look up how far I traveled to each appointment for each way.

Luckily in this new era, you have several apps to choose from that make the tracking process so much easier and functional.

Some apps offer a free version or a trial period before being charged the monthly fee to continue using the operating system. Opting to upgrade and pay for the tracking software apps that offer a free plan, is a good option in the long run as you will have full access to all the software's functions.

The following are my top picks of mileage tracking apps in the industry:

1. QuickBooks Self-Employed
2. SherpaShare
3. Hurdlr
4. Everlance
5. MileTracker

You will also be able to write off the fees you paid for mileage tracking and financial management software on your return and utilizing these types of software can ease the tax filing process.

"Someone's sitting in the shade today because someone planted a tree a long time ago."

Warren Buffett

COMMUNICATION

You must have a working and reliable phone and communication systems in place, in order to properly structure booking and building your business effectively.

SAFETY

Take the proper measures to initially interview and pre-screen a potential massage client you do not know or was not referred to you by someone you know as thoroughly as possible. If you're not able to meet in person, have a list of questions to get an overall assessment of the person prior to officially booking the session.

Key questions you need to ask:

▶ First & Last name?

▶ Address session will be performed at? Also, whether it's a residence or business, and who else is expected to be at the session?

▶ If you are scared or allergic to certain animals, or just like knowing that information, you may want to ask if they have pets?

For clients who have pets that shed a lot, I like having a lint brush in the car to remove any hair that may stick to me. I also am allergic to cats, so knowing there will be cats present, I can make sure I take allergy medicine in advance to reduce my allergic reaction.

▶ How was he/she was referred to you?

▶ Who is their employer and what physical demands are required for their job that are potentially affecting their ailments?

▶ Then do a full intake on what client's problem areas are, if they have had previous surgeries or if they have any hardware in their body, why they are wanting a session and when their last massage was?

Ask questions in any order you see fit and continue to inquire for additional information important to you in pre-screening a potential client. You want to have the conversation flow naturally, and not be robotic or too rehearsed while gaining information received to verify a client's identity. You will be surprised of the assessment you can get and what you can learn in one conversation with a person.

I attempt to search information as I'm receiving it online during my pre-screen process. If I'm still unsure about doing the session, or unable to search while I'm talking with them, I'll ask what days and times they were thinking of getting worked on and if I can follow-up with them within a few hours.

I'll explain that I currently have clients scheduled but have not confirmed for those days, so I can give accurate times I may be available once hearing from them.

After hanging up I will go online and do a Google search with the information I was provided with. If there is no web presence for the individual, disturbing information about the potential client is found, or when doing an address search comes back as a sketchy or a bogus address, I will not book the session. Paying attention to additional information a client may disclose about themselves, such as them having kids, marital status or even if they have a pet, can assist you in the verification process if you come across multiple social media profiles with the similar name.

If you opt to continue booking the appointment, attempt to schedule it in the morning or afternoon until you become comfortable with a client. Additionally, let your closest friends and/or family know what client you're going to, so they can follow-up with you and make sure you're ok after the session is complete. I have been on the phone with someone, and while in front of the new client, will tell who I'm talking to that I just arrived at the session I was telling them about and will call when I finish. That lets the person know that they were discussed and at least one person knows your current whereabouts.

If a client requests to extend their current session and you agree, tell them if you can make a quick call to let your friend or whoever know you're staying later than planned so they won't go crazy and put and A.P.B out on you if they call and you do not answer. Again, letting the client know people are monitoring your whereabouts which is a good deterrent if they had bad intentions in mind.

At the end of the day, you must trust your gut feeling and intuition and use common sense if you don't feel comfortable at any time. Remember you have the power to not book or terminate a session at any point.

PHONE

I'm not only old school but also OCD about my scheduling and time, so I book all my appointments thru text or phone and use my phones calendar to input my appointments, and I have my phone and calendar synced with my Gmail account. Having your contact list and everything in your calendar synced with your email and cloud, is important in the event your phone breaks, gets stolen or lost. Once a new phone is obtained, and you program your email to your phone, all the information will be imported onto the new phone.

I have had to restart with all new contacts and lost all my scheduling information, so you must have a systemization that works for you to ensure this doesn't happen. The process can be stressful, and if this happens to you, make a custom voicemail message asking callers to leave name and contact information because you've lost all contact and scheduling information. You can also post on your social networks and ask for everyone to direct message you their contact info.

EMAIL

Gmail is my favorite email platform, you can also use a custom email associated with your webpage once it's all setup. Pick an email format that is professional, you don't want to use a name that's totally unrelated or not in line with your company structure. I have had individuals reach out to me and the email addresses used to discuss business is quite laughable.

Also, if you are networking and working with corporations, they will be more inclined to do business with you if this simple rule is followed.

Gmail also offers the "google voice" option once email is created which will allow you to create and setup a free phone number to attach to your current cell phone service. Very helpful to protect your privacy, eliminate/block unwanted calls, and to separate and distinguish work calls, voicemails and texts from your personal ones if you are wanting to separate the two. Privacy, safety and cost are top reasons to accept this option, and why pay for an additional phone and phone line when you can get one for free while managing it all from one device.

SCHEDULING SOFTWARE

Although I do not use any scheduling software, Vagaro, Genbook and StyleSeat are popular options amongst my friends in the industry. Make sure when setting your appointment parameters within your scheduling software, that you take into account enough travel time between sessions and anticipate any events that could cause a delay in your arrival time;

such as weather, potential traffic due to high peak hours or a special event going on in the area during certain dates and times.

Appointments that could potentially get booked during peak traffic periods, should minimally have an additional 15 - 20 minutes added onto the standard time allotted between session times to offset any setbacks. You would hate to have your whole day off track because of delays arriving to your session on time.

Most of these applications can be embedded or added to your webpage, and most scheduling software can act as its own website in the event you don't have one setup yet.

WEBSITE

Before your site can be built, the first thing you need to do is go buy a web domain. GoDaddy is a popular choice for this step. Choose your website domain, choose specifications of domain, how many years you want to pay for domain, and finalize the order. You can choose to pay one year at a time, or 5 or 10 years upfront if you think you will forget to renew the domain once it's about to expire. GoDaddy will send email reminders once the expiration time is coming near, but if you fail to renew your domain and it expires, your website will be down.

Next you will need to build your webpage and there are so many platforms where you can create a website on your own at a very reasonable fee, like Wix, Weebly and WordPress, just to name a few. The best benefit is you can set the site up to your specifications and can update and change it as often and anytime you choose without having to depend and be at a web designers mercy.

Input and set-up the general format of your site with all the content and photos of how you would like the flow of your page to go, and at this point if you're still not fully happy with the look of your site, bring in a web designer to clean-up and make your site more professional looking. This route is a cost-effective tip because the site isn't being built from scratch.

When I did this, I changed the password for my site and GoDaddy temporarily, (web designer will need passwords to the domain and website to link everything), to something else and changed it back once they were complete. Doing this still gives you full control of your website and then you still have the ability to go in and add and make changes when necessary.

I have had friends over the years who have fallen out with a web designer and their whole site was not only built by the web designer, but the site was also being hosted on their server, so the whole process to transfer all their content and switch hosting could be lengthy and messy process. Using this method removes all those headaches and frustrations and if you choose to use a web designer, they can have access to your account to do their job, while maintaining full control of your content the entire time.

As a therapist, you won't have a ton of updates to make. I usually log on to add photos to my site, but the great thing about site building platforms is that you can add your social media account links, blog, store, YouTube, etc. to your site so all your content will automatically update as you post and use it.

LISTEN AND ADJUST

Chemistry with a client is important so listening and adjusting your technique are factors to achieving that. As they express what their issues are, really pay attention to their body mechanics as you are working on them.

It's easy to get caught up in their conversation, or just flat out be in day-dream mode but being focused and as attentive as possible are fundamental to a successful session. This applies to not only new clients, but even to clients you have retained for repeat service.

Bad session inquiry

When a client tells me they've had a bad massage experience in the past, I typically ask why? First to get pointers for myself so I don't repeat any behavior or techniques that caused their previous bad experience. Also, to give them insight on ways they can handle and view the situation if it was to happen again, as the typical reaction is to just write off that therapist.

Two of the leading complaints in all my years of massage are either:

    (1) They felt worse the day after the massage session.
    (2) Felt the therapist was not listening to their requests and verbal ques.

× *Specifically regarding technique, because hopefully the tips and recommendations throughout the book will assist dodging more personal reasons a client would have disliked the session.*

I ask if at any point during the massage did they ask the therapist to adjust their pressure or let them know what they were doing was causing them pain? When the answer is "No," I slightly go into massage therapist defense

mode and explain that although a therapist potentially works on the human body almost daily, they are not mind readers! The fact that there is a different body on their table every time they work means they must make various adjustments to each client as everyone has varying issues and personal likes and dislikes during a session.

I am naturally heavy-handed and sometimes don't realize my strength, so I would have no clue if a client, who shows no signs verbally or physically would choose to just lay there and bare any discomfort I'm not intending to administer. I communicate ahead of time any techniques that I know will cause a little discomfort or pain, but insist they inform me if it's too much to tolerate.

Keep in mind I typically do very detailed fascia work, so the techniques I perform are not traditional in nature. Which is why I make it a priority to communicate ahead of time and explain what I'm about to do and what they should expect. This also sets the client at ease that you are fully aware of your actions and allows them to relax and trust the process.

Whether you are performing a specialty type of massage or doing a Swedish massage, create an environment open for communication and to receive feedback.

Post massage pain

For clients that felt "beat-up" the day after the massage and felt as if they were hit by a car, I most always suggest they should have iced. Moving forward, anytime someone gets worked on, including yourself, and has signs of soreness and pain as the day progresses, should consider having an ice bath or at least placing ice-packs in the areas requiring treatment.

This will keep from excessive inflammation setting in after a massage, which is one of the causes of soreness and pain and not necessarily because a therapist did something wrong. The iced areas may still be tender to touch the following day, but at least the initial onset of inflammation can subside, and I explain the process may need to be repeated for a few days following an intense therapy session.

Importance of maintaining boundaries

Now a big no-no and an act that's hard to defend, is when a client states they made attempts to communicate but the therapist didn't accommodate and adapt to what was being said. If a client communicates that what you are doing is uncomfortable or painful, or simply requests more pressure, and either you never or for only a short time adjust your pressure during the session, that's an issue. I've even had client's mention therapist forcing them to follow thru with a therapy technique they could not tolerate or was not comfortable with.

Even though your intention is to help and heal your client and you can see and feel what should be done, that may not always be attainable in that session.

Furthermore, a client may never get to that point, but at no time should any approach towards their care be forced or beyond the boundaries they are comfortable with.

I have a handful of clients that outright say, "Joann I know my body is fucked up, but I don't want you to fix me… I just want to relax and feel good right now." Even though I know their immediate results are temporary, I must respect their boundaries and strive to give them the result they desire for the session.

At the end of the day you are in the service industry and a client is choosing to pay you for that service when they could have gone to someone else. So, whether you agree with the therapeutic method, or even if your skill set isn't advanced enough to give them the result they want, explain why you are suggesting your approach or your inability to do something. Choosing to gradually allow the client's body to acclimate to your method within their comfort zone, is the best long-term option rather than pushing them beyond their limits.

Also, client's will most likely respect your honesty if you say you haven't been trained or have not built up the endurance to perform a requested technique, but you will attempt to give them what they are wanting to the best of your ability. Rather than saying you can do something and totally miss the mark, which can be received as you ignoring their request since you are unable to make the proper adjustments.

☼ Tip

Be sure to make clients feel comfortable to express how they feel at any point in the session and that doing so will not insult or bother you in any way, as you want them to have the most gratifying experience possible. Also create a "finish move" for the end of your massage. I like to end with a neck, scalp and/or temple massage to soothe and relax the client at the end of a session but inquire and spend time on an area of the body they enjoy the most.

"Knowledge will give you power, but

character respect."

Bruce Lee

BE STRUCTURED, BUT FLEXIBLE...

A major key to my success, besides being pretty F'in' fabulous as a person and skilled at my craft, is the fact that I have major insomnia. I've suffered from insomnia from a very young age and have self-diagnosed myself and credit Freddy Krueger and the whole Nightmare on Elm Street movies for my condition, but that's a whole other book topic. So, although not very beneficial for my personal being, I utilized what most would accept as a disadvantage and was able to grow and build an extensive client base from it.

Most clients want to get worked on after work and in the evening, preferably once kids are fed and put to bed, and before they themselves plan to go to sleep. In knowing this fact, I did not have a cutoff hour of when I would not work. Since most of my clients are doctors, athletes and musicians, this factor comes in very handy, as I've went to someone's home at midnight or 1am before. The average person may not understand this concept, but within the medical, sports and entertainment field, this is very common.

During my peak seasons, and on the busiest days, I will start at roughly 1pm and not finish working until 1am – 2am. There is only one of me, so I must plan what order I'm going to each client and typically like to book client's that live in the same area and work my way in towards my home.

Doesn't always work out that way, but I attempt to structure the scheduling in that way to reduce excessive back and forth traveling and reduce gas.

†

You could be working backstage for an artist and they may want to get worked on after the show, the only catch is, most of the time they may have an appearance or must do some sort of media following their performance, so there have been times I'm starting on a massage session at two or three in the morning. Again, abnormal for the average person to comprehend, but very common practice in this industry, but the good thing is you have the option to add an additional fee on top of your normal rate as a massage at that hour is an added amenity you are providing. In these situations, and depending on the time, I will add an additional $50 - $75 fee on top of my normal rate.

Choosing to add an extra rate is up to you, but a good rule of thumb when booking these type of massage gigs is stating your fee structure upfront, so no one feels like you're trying to get over and overcharge for the session. For example, my normal rate is $125 an hour and the rate quoted would be good from the time I arrive at the venue until midnight; any massages after that time would be at $175 or $200 an hour.

I would choose the rate based on the distance the venue was from my home, what my work schedule was the following day and if I gave the person booking the gig a deal on backstage massages. Depending on what show it was, I would choose a set hourly rate of $60 - $80 an hour or charge $1 - $2 a minute for anyone wanting massage or stretching backstage, and the service is available to artist, dancers and crew.

There have even been a few times where I've adjusted and lowered my pricing a little because I got along so well with the crew, artist and management so enjoying the moment, getting to know everyone and creating good networking connections has paid off over my career because they refer their friends and colleagues to me when they come in town. Making sure you are being compensated for your services is important and I by no means am advising anyone to work for free or way below their worth, I'm just saying that accessing the environment and potential work relationships you can make can be a factor in not only establishing your name, but also obtaining future business.

Whichever niche field of massage you decide to go with, don't be apprehensive to go beyond what some perceive as standard, and think and work outside the box. Especially if you observe the strategy you have in place is effective and best suits a client's needs.

Seeing as I knew I would be up late nights anyway, why not be making money and connections instead of being home looking up at the ceiling and trying to fall asleep.

This has been lucrative financially and even if clients don't use the late session option, it does great for building client retention because they know they have that option available. So, I turned my insomnia lemon into some pretty amazing lemonade!

"When you want to succeed as bad as you want to breathe, then you'll be successful."

Eric Thomas

ACCEPTING PAYMENTS AND PRICING

When you first start out, you need to research the massage market in your area.

When stating pricing to anyone throughout your practice, it's better to start at a rate you feel is your worth and comfortable with, especially if the client does not tip on top of the price you have in place. Even if your skill-set is above average but are new to the business and are focused on building your clientele, you can set your base rate and offer specials, discounts and offer a loyalty program in the beginning, until you are more established.

Best Options to Accept Payment for Services:

Cash

You can never go wrong with cash, Cash is King and best option.

Check

Clients will use a personal or business check written to you personally or in your business name for payment of services. There is no extra fee to deposit check in your account.

Charge

Square and PayPal are popular options to setup for processing credit card payments. These credit card processing options do not charge a monthly fee to utilize them, but they do take a small percentage when a charge is made. You can manually input, use chip or swipe feature, but the fee is more if you manually input a payment.

I charge an additional credit card processing fee ($5) on top of the massage rate when the client picks this as their payment method. Whatever processing system you choose will take a percentage of each sell, so I add the fee as to not take away from my profit margin. This is just a suggestion but choose a fee that best suits your price structure and market. I have seen therapist charge anywhere from $3 - $10 for single session charges, but if you offer packages for bulk session purchases, you may want to think about having a separate credit card fee for this option because the credit card processing fee will be higher than normal.

Again, having or upping your set credit card fee is not necessary, but if you choose to add a credit card fee and if the said fee could change if they choose to buy sessions in bulk, please have the fee stated in the beginning. No one wants last minute fees taxed on without prior notice.

Digital

Zelle, Venmo, PayPal or CashApp – most favorable digital options to send and receive money.

You can post all accepted forms of payment on your website and social media outlets.

ESTABLISHING PAY RATE & TIPS WHEN TRAVELING FOR A CLIENT

Pay Rate

Thoroughly research your competition and see what the going rate for a mobile massage is in your market. Once you establish the lowest and highest rates, study what modalities are marketed and see if there is a lack in an area you feel you can offer and excel in. Once you've completed all your market research, sit back and give yourself an honest evaluation of where your skill set is at and rate yourself.

This step is very important, so be very honest with yourself because if you enter the market with sub-par or average technique, but then are demanding top tier payment, you can damage your long-term client retention. As you grow as a therapist and invest in your training and tools, don't hesitate to increase your rate. Your clients will take notice and want to remain with you because they will observe you're only getting better, are invested in your craft and will see the demand for you increase overtime as a result.

A recommendation I can give for a starting base range is $55 - $90 an hour. Whether you feel your technique is great or you want to feel out the market and quickly build clientele, this price range is fair for a mobile therapist starting out. My initial massage rate when I began was $65 an hour, but as my massage abilities improved and I gained more clientele, my hourly rate has increased to $125 - $150 an hour. Keeping education and tool investments, gas, mileage, car maintenance, and overall travel (i.e. traffic, hours spent in car, etc.) have also contributed to my rate. I do charge an additional $25 fee if I must travel over 25 - 30 miles to a session.

At this point in my career I feel I am the best in the industry and feel I could charge more, but I'm not driven by greed and am very comfortable with the rate I'm at for now. Once you are fully confident in your artistry, do not let anyone make you feel bad for the rate you know you're worth. Because 20 - 30 years from now if you get arthritis or pain in your limbs as a result of all your hard work, the last thing you want to say to yourself when you look back at your career, is you wish you would have charged more.

Set Goals

Sit down and list all your monthly living expenses and calculate in your potential leisure budget as well. This will give you an idea of how many sessions will need to be done to reach your required goal. For example, if you need to make $800 a week and say your massage rate is $80 an hour, then you know you'll need to minimally perform 10 hours of massage a week at your normal rate to reach this goal. Setting, maintaining and surpassing your goals will keep you financially on track.

Specials

During slow times and/or to stay consistently busy, consider running specials from time to time. You can use your social media, email and texting to inform clients you are offering discounted rates for said time. After working on clients, you can even offer them discounted sessions if they pre-book 1 - 2 sessions ahead of time.

For example, if your normal rate is $100 an hour, you can offer $70 sessions for appointments booked during a particular time frame. Or say you charge $150 for a 90-minute session, you can offer a $90 for 90-minute session or any price you are comfortable offering for a specific day or period of time.

Occasionally I will offer specials on massage packages, usually ranging from 5 -10 sessions. You can choose to take a specific percentage off bulk sessions or offer 90 - minute packages for the price of an hour package rate. The great thing is you are in control of your pricing structure so be creative, and find what works best for you, your schedule and work capability.

Traveling with Table

When I work out of town, I really do not like bringing my table, especially if I'm going to their home as opposed to a location they are at temporarily. I either have a client order one on their own, especially if massage if something they do often, or I can order an affordable table for them off eBay or Amazon, have it shipped to their location and they can pay me before I order or once I arrive. A client typically opts to buy the table, since the airline bag fee is added to the cost of travel so since they're paying for it anyways, it just makes since for them to buy it, rather than throw that money away.

Roughly the starting baggage fee is $50 - $100 each way to travel with a massage table (depending on the weight and dimensions), and as stated earlier in the *supplies chapter*, an above average table online can range between $125 - $199 so you see why most opt to purchase one.

If for example I'm going to a location for 3 or more days to work on one or several clients and have advance notice I'll be traveling; I will order a table, have it sent to the hotel and then put it on Craigslist or similar site to sell it at the price I purchased it at or a little cheaper to dump it fast before leaving town. In the event I cannot sell it, then I'm only paying for the shipping for one-way and I sell it when I get home.

If you choose to travel with any massage tools, it's a good idea to carry-on the most important and expensive ones in your carry-on baggage. Any tool that has a lithium battery is advised to carry-on anyways. For example, I always bring my cupping set, one of my small Gua Sha tools and Hypervolt device in my backpack.

If you were a traveling barber, you wouldn't check your barber kit in with your luggage, it would go on the plane with you because if your luggage got lost or delayed getting to you, how can you work?

Luckily in massage, your hands are your most important tool, but any modality that enhances your craft you wouldn't want to work without.

☼ Tip

If you're a therapist with a heavy aluminum table like myself and must travel with your own table; it would be a good option to have a lightweight wooden table to use for travel purposes. Also put massage lubricant in TSA approved bottle in carry-on.

Establishing Travel Pay Rate & Schedule

It's good to establish a day rate, and that day rate needs to be based on several factors. Not including travel, how many clients will be getting worked on, how many hours a day and what the client's needs, and goals are while you're there. Also, the time of year plays a factor for me as well. I will charge roughly $500 - $850 a day depending on what's currently booked on my schedule when a client requests for me to travel.

During high-peak times of the year for me like the NFL season, I will charge $1000 - $1500 a day as I will be losing a great deal of income, with potential to lose clients as a result of me opting to travel. So, the gain must be slightly more than the potential loss during times like this, but each scenario is assessed individually to come up with a rate that works for all parties.

Having great communication with your clients is imperative to retaining them upon your return. I am honest and let them all know before booking that there is a possibility I may have to leave during certain periods, so if in fact it happens, they may be disappointed but are not upset with me when I must alter the schedule. As an amenity and courtesy, I do have a small network of therapist I source work out to if clients are needing a more immediate appointment in my absence.

†

For flight and/or hotel bookings, either the client themselves, the client's assistant or rep will usually contact me to book travel arrangements and will email me my travel details. If a client is within driving distance, I will drive and add a travel fee (usually between $150 - $300) on top of the total massage fee. This rate is based on the distance it takes to get to location. I will also check current flight rates as another tool to help come up with my travel fee and evaluate the savings with me driving to them. The furthest I have driven for a client was roughly 5.5 hours.

My client did not live in this city but was training there and I stayed in town a little over a week to work. So, driving there made more sense and was the most cost-effective way to get me to the city. The luxury of this option is you can take more massage gear and personal items without worrying about security or baggage and luggage weight fees at the airport and I had the freedom of going anywhere as needed on my downtime since I had my vehicle.

Sample of how I like to setup my schedule

Inquire the client's schedule for the day and duration of the time you're there. You want to map out not only potential massage and stretch times, but also if you can fit in other activities while you're in town, which I will explain.

Several factors I look at while with a client:

If they workout, I go to the session and observe the clients body mechanics while working out, and if I observe slight things that can be corrected, I will suggest when appropriate and not to step on a trainer's toes if the client happens to be working with one. I am not a trainer, so I stay in my lane when it comes to other individuals craft, but sometimes, they may not notice or even know to be observing certain areas that need to be corrected that you know have been problem areas for them during a massage session.

When and if I want to suggest something to a client at the time of their training session, I will first communicate with the trainer and let them know what I'm noticing and why I'm suggesting or correcting any movements because you want to work together for the betterment of your client, not work against each other.

I continue to see how those body mechanics change throughout the day, and I pay attention to their hydration levels. Some clients may feel they hydrate enough, but if they did a long workout, are outside in the elements or been on the go for the duration of the day, then 8 – 10 glasses or less of water may not be enough to maintain proper hydration levels.

Research Options in Their Area

If a client is open to it, I will look into scheduling a consultation with a nutritionist and maybe even a chef to help setup a proper food regimen specifically tailored for them. I will also research yoga and pilates classes we could attend as those are the top exercises I suggest for foundational stability for the body.

Booking recovery sessions such as cryotherapy, drip spa or at a float tank facility and finding a physician that can perform acupuncture and adjustments are also some great recovery methods to educate your client on. You want your client to be as fully informed as possible and comfortable to trying these methods out before you leave, so they can continue this after your departure.

In my regular business practice, I like to explain and inform clients of not only their concerns, but also what I see can benefit them moving forward. When traveling, I may go a little overboard with the information because I know my time and their accessibility to me is limited, so I want them to have all the information I can think of which I feel also makes the money spent on me commuting to them worth the investment. So, keep this in mind when choosing to travel for your client's and take the time to go that extra mile researching beneficial options that will compliment a massage session.

RECEIPT AND INVOICES

Buy a receipt book and create receipt and invoice templates. I bring the receipt book to my backstage gigs or events I'm unsure may request one, as I won't have a laptop and printer on hand to whip one up. On the receipt book, I have pre-made, address label size stickers, with the company logo and website on each receipt. A custom receipt book can be created through companies like deluxe.com or printpps.com, but since I don't use this method often I opted to create and place the stickers on each one (in color) because it was the cheapest option for me that maintained a professional look.

Most business or event functions will require an invoice for their records to pay for massage services rendered, so you want to have all your business information, negotiated rates and hours, with the total due and most importantly, who the check is to be made out to and where the check is to be mailed if that is the payment method. In some cases, it will take 2 – 4 weeks for the company to process and mail you your check after receiving the invoice.

Also keep good records in the event a client wants a receipt for the entire year to submit for a tax deduction.

"We are in control of the one asset that we all give the most fucks about, and that is time."

Gary Vaynerchuk

MARKETING

EXPLORE AND FIND YOUR NICHE MARKET

My "niche market" is a sports and fascia therapist, but someone may want to focus on energy work or even consider becoming a doula. Once you have your main niche market, this doesn't mean you can't veer from it when requested, but establish the main market you not only want to focus on, but also thrive in. For example, I had a car wreck years ago and was having some TMJ issues (something I've never experienced before). The therapist I was referred to did some amazing work inside of my mouth, also something I never experienced before. This area of massage isn't something I've ever been interested in performing or gaining a vast array of knowledge on, but this technique was very effective and resolved my issue.

BUSINESS CARDS

Create a contact card – In your cellphone create a contact card with all pertinent business info, and include the following:

° Phone #   ° Email   ° Website

° Social Media Handles

° Date of Birth (optional)

Doing this is an easy way for you to forward your information to people you meet and/or when someone wants to refer clients to you. So, your contact card you create in your phone is basically your virtual business card.

PROMOTIONAL ITEMS

Excellent when marketing to business' and wanting to leave items to remind them they should book with you. You can create items like clothing, notepads, pens, stress balls, magnets or cups. A marketing company was having a special on mini swiss army pocket knives, so I had my company name and website on them. Anything you feel a potential client will keep and use as a constant reminder they should book you.

SOCIAL MEDIA

Social Media is Gold when used productively and correctly:

Social media is one of the best forms of mass marketing for your business in this day in age. Facebook, Twitter, Instagram, YouTube, LinkedIn, SnapChat and Pinterest are leading the list of social media and marketing platforms. Study and research hashtags relative to your target market and use popular ones to draw traffic to your social media pages. Even create a few hashtags that you can create as unique markers for yourself so as you gain a following, when someone clicks on it sees content specifically related to your business.

On Instagram, my unique hashtags are #MassageNinja and #TherapistToTheStars. Recently, people are beginning to use the #MassageNinja & #TherapistToTheStars hashtags more, but if you look at all the posts relating to it, you'll see I was one of the first to ever post using them for a while. Although people are posting using the hashtags, you will see my business content have the greatest presence. In addition to those two hashtags, I will post popular ones along with it, like #Massage #Cupping #Swim or #Boxing for example, to complement my post.

I use hashtags to correlate with what content I'm posting so I will mix main stream hashtags with my designated ones created for my brand. Once your business continues to grow or when you do any events, or on your marketing material, you can have your catchy unique hashtags as a way to promote and brand your business and ask your clients to use them when posting and tagging content.

†

Creating, editing and posting on all social media sites can be very time consuming and I see why companies have a whole division that focuses on managing those postings on all outlets. This area of the business I struggle with from time to time, especially during busy work seasons throughout the year because my focus is more on my work performance rather than the social media aspect.

For those of you that can juggle your work schedule, while posting good content for your business, this skill will be key in building and establishing a true online presence at a faster rate. Just make sure your systems are in place and ready for the growth if our posting tactics draw business to you in record numbers. If you need a little preparation to establish what methods work best for you, take your time and ease into marketing on social media outlets. I've always preferred quality over quantity as it relates to any business, and I always wanted to make sure I was prepared before excelling to the next level, rather than get opportunities and fail, and then who knows if I would have been given that chance again. Me opting for the slower route for years regarding social media postings for business took time, but my foundation is strong and now I don't have to market very hard to obtain new massage business. People find me or are referred to me as a result of all the ground work I've put in personally by going out and meeting people at events and functions organically over the years.

†

Social media wasn't as strong over 10 years ago, so for the new generation of therapist I advise using these platforms, coupled with some old school methods to establish and build your brand.

In saying that, what you post on your media platforms can greatly enhance or kill your chance of gaining the type of clientele you desire. For example, posting you partying all the time, half naked photos, personal venting sessions about your private life; or even overzealous political views one way or another, can affect you obtaining a client or chances of cross promoting with other people.

I personally have not responded to messages, referred business or will agree to mentor other therapist because I felt their intentions of truly wanting to learn and grow weren't authentic, and lead me to believe they just wanted to be around the type of clientele I had. This assumption could have been farther from the truth, but perception and first impressions are what people see before getting the opportunity to speak and get to know you.

When you are choosing to use the internet as your primary method to market for business, be sure to keep these few points in mind... especially before reaching out in efforts to cross-promote with individuals and companies.

I'm not saying you can't mix in personal posts with your work content, because I do, you just want to make sure your craft outshines everything else. So, keep this important theme in line when creating and posting for your personal and business pages, because everything you post on social media is available for the world to see FOREVER.

☼ Tip

If you desire more freedom with social media postings, set-up "private" personal pages for friends and family only, and "public" business pages specifically for marketing your business and communicating with potential clients. For instance, my personal Facebook page is the only social media account that I have private because its more intimate for me.

HOTEL & HIGHRISES

Some hotels will hire therapist on an on-call basis only, so look into applying as that doesn't require you to commit to a set schedule and can be an extra revenue stream if they call and you are available.

When you leave any hotel or high rise, tip valet attendant, and give them a few cards. If the location has a concierge, introduce yourself, chat with them for a few minutes and tell them what you do and your specialties and give them a few cards and tip them as well because guests usually will ask them if they can refer a therapist that would come to their room to do a massage. Even offer the concierge or valet attendant a discount you're comfortable with if they refer business.

NETWORKING 101

Utilize the connections you already have, and you can even start this process in the last phase of massage school. When you are performing the required hands-on sessions in order apply and take your state's massage exam for your license, begin reaching out to your phone contact list.

You can build a book of clientele in this phase that would be happily waiting to be your client once you obtain your massage license. So, tell your family, friends, and friends of friends to come see you during this time because it's the cheapest rate they can experience a massage from you.

My friends and work connections from my clinic were what initially jump started my client base. When your family and friends believe and use your services, it speaks volumes to the quality of work you provide.

It only takes one client referral to take your business to the next level, and many high-profile clients I've obtained were from my friends and referrals from past clients.

When I voiced I wanted to build my professional athlete clientele list, I was fortunate to have current clients invite me to parties and functions to put me in positions to network and build my business. Depending on the market you want to get into, its always a good option to have someone that's familiar or knows your target market to give you the introduction. This is a great vetting system for you and your business.

Same goes for maybe networking with physicians or even asking friends that work for companies you would like to offer your chair massage services to, to guide you to the contact person and assist in getting you that initial introduction with their employer.

Encouraging your family and friends to refer your contact info to people they know may want your service, is also an additional safeguard since there is someone linking you with a new client unknown to you personally.

†

If you have no connections, then create the opportunities. I'm a people person and enjoy talking and meeting just about anyone, and I always have business cards on me to pass out if the energy the individual(s) I'm speaking with is positive. Look up events you want to go to, whether that be massage or business conferences, seminars or charity events.

Take advantage of meeting and cross-promoting with other therapist in your area and even in other states and internationally when possible. I have therapist in other states and countries and when I have a client needing to get worked on in their area, I'll refer them business and they will do the same when their clients are in my area.

There are also many groups you can join to meet and assist in establishing the connections you want. Look into local social groups like meetup.com for example, and there are even global networking organizations that require an annual fee and some even a referral from a current member to join (i.e.: FoundersCard, Dynamite Circle to name a few). A major advantage in belonging to these groups is they have special offers for hotels, travel, lifestyle and business services, and events. The opportunity to network with other likeminded entrepreneurs across the globe can be an asset for getting advice and building your business.

†

If I knew an athlete, performer or popular public figure was throwing a party, having a meet and greet or charity event, I would go to see if I could connect with someone in their camp.

Key thing in these situations, is not to be an annoyance or come off "creepy." If access to an athlete or entertainer is difficult, see if you can network with a rep (i.e.: manager or personal assistant, etc.) or even the bodyguard.

If you wanted to be a Doula, a good strategy would be going to parenting classes and meeting instructors, going to maternity stores and even building a network of OB/Gyn doctors that could send you business.

I would go to various functions to get my name out and to create opportunities for myself, but it's also something I love because networking and meeting people is a fun process for me. Networking in any trade is vital to growth, so be the King or Queen of whatever market you choose to target.

CHAIR MASSAGE EVENTS

HR managers, secretaries or personal assistants for businesses are typically the go to contact person to pitch the idea of offering chair massages to employees or their clients. Most employers like the idea of having a therapist come into the business as an employee appreciation gift.

Some would have a therapist come once or twice a year, or even quarterly if they have the budget for it. Companies that have gym access in their building are great targets as health and fitness are obviously important in their company structure and some may even get a tax and insurance break for bringing a therapist in periodically to reduce employee stress and boost employee mood, morale and energy level.

Keep in mind that even if the event is booked as a "chair massage" function, certain scenarios will be better suited to bring a table instead of the chair or may want the option for both.

†

You can even market your massage services to high rises and apartment complexes. Go to the leasing office and offer a resident relaxation day as most complexes offer functions once a month or every quarter for their residents. In these situations, it would be a good idea to know 1 - 3 more therapist if they would desire multiple therapist to accommodate all the residents that come to the event.

If you do not know any other therapist, it would be good to network with other business' in the health and wellness field that could also come and add to a resident event. Examples would be trainers, a meal prep company or juicing company that can offer samples and discount cards for their services but get creative with cross promoting options.

Chair massage rates can vary anywhere from $30 - $100 an hour per therapist depending on how long they desire the massage services and how many therapists are working the event. Having a 2 - hour minimum for any booked chair massage event is standard and would be more worth your time and energy and have a tip jar handy if the client allows you to accept them.

Some business' will opt not for you to accept tips because they do not want their residents paying anything and would rather add the tip on top of the rate.

Music Festivals

This usually involves an outdoor concert with a roster of different performing acts throughout the day and the venue usually has more than one stage to alternate between acts and allow setup time for the next one. These events can be fun, especially if the lineup includes people you enjoy listening to. The downside is, there's not a lot of money typically for this option.

These events have varying scales of tickets that can be purchased, and they usually like to setup therapist in the VIP area as an added amenity for those that purchased VIP status. Also, your payment is usually a set number of those VIP bands for your services. So basically, you are getting wrist bands for the show and working for tips as payment.

If one is willing to work, you can make a decent amount of money on tips, so don't get too bummed thinking there isn't anything to be made. For these events I will ask at least 2 therapists to work with me, and request at least 6 – 8 bands total. The key is to work a lot in the beginning when the smaller acts are performing, and then 30 – 45 minutes before the last 2 acts go on or when the crowd diminishes, begin the breakdown process and pack up and load your things so you can enjoy the last shows.

It's also a good idea to alternate with the therapist prior, so you all can survey the area and get a feel of the event before the headlining acts come on stage. I do love working these events because I enjoy music and concerts and they really are fun, which is why I still choose to do them when the opportunity arises even though the monetary factor is minimal.

Trade Shows

Unlike festivals, you usually must pay a fee to join a trade show. Depending on the event, the booth price may vary depending on the size of booth you desire. Since you are paying for space, you can charge for anyone wanting to use any services you are offering.

Again, I will go in with 1 – 4 therapists on booth fee and the supplies and we will alternate shifts. I also will sell products like Biofreeze, stress balls and will even do paraffin wraps for hands. Anything to add to the revenue stream for the time you are setup, as you will be surprised how the money will add up. Doing this also allows for additional services to be performed while someone is waiting to get worked on.

Be creative with trade shows too and don't think it has to only fall into the health and wellness field. One of my most profitable trade shows in my career was at a boat show. The boat show was for a week and our booth made over $7,000 and I did it with only one other therapist.

I believe our booth fee, with supplies cost was about $500 - $600, so the profit we made was worth the investment. It was tiring and required us to work a bit, but we were very happy with the outcome and the connections that were made once it was all over.

Booth Supplies and Setup

Primary supplies for festivals or trade shows, would be a lot of paper towels, Clorox wipes and business cards. Some added marketing tools would be a banner for the table and/or backdrop to enhance your booth as well as giving away samples of any marketing materials or therapeutic items you have.

Law School

One of my chair massage gigs I have had for several years is for a law school. The school pays for me to come in and massage the students during finals time, three times a week, five hours on each day, for two weeks. That one company brings me almost $2,000 for 30 hours of work. Envision having a few of these booked a month, in addition to the revenue you bring in with your house calls.

Do you have a nursing or medical school in your area, police, fire stations, or even military base? All these and more are options to be open to.

☼ Tip

For a chair massage gig that's booked for several days and hours, should have a structured scheduling system to allow booking for the current and future dates you will be there. A free option, but useful app is VolunteerSpot (www.SignUp.com). You can create custom sign-in sheets for each day, and it even has the ability to send reminders to everyone who has signed up. I'm sure there may be more options, but this has worked for me.

Typically for a one-day corporate chair massage event, after we negotiate pay rate, and time for each massage, I'll ask them to make a sign-in sheet prior to me arriving and having everyone sign-up in their desired time slot. They usually will hang it outside of the area I'm setup to massage.

Small Towns

If you live in a rural area, do not think there are no opportunities for growth. I'm originally from a small town in West Texas, and we're mostly known for high school football and oil and gas. If I were to move back home to work now, I obviously would market to all the oil and gas companies, but I would go one step further and offer to go onsite at an oil rig to work on employees.

Most of them will stay and work onsite from one to two weeks, working a 10 – 12 hour day shift. It's not only exhausting, but very dangerous and demanding on one's body, as being alert, aware and as rested as possible are factors to a safe workday. The rig could be 30 minutes to over an hour or two away, but if I were to pitch the idea, I would add hotel and gas in the budget if necessary and say I could come for 1 – 2 full days to ensure I could work on the majority employees for all shifts and to make their investment worth the time.

†

I also would market to the minor league team and high school and junior college athletes. One thing parents of athletes, and some small and collegiate organization will do is spend money on their talent. I have a whole swim group ranging from middle school to high school as clients. I gave them a discount off my normal rate, and with the number of clients gained, was worth the price cut.

The same can be done in any area, and once you get a few clients and perform first-rate massage and stretching sessions, the word will get out that you are a therapist who is worth the expense.

One last suggestion would be to consider marketing to horse breeders, stables or anywhere equestrian training is performed. Riders, trainers and stable staff could be potential clients. Whether they just breed or are into using them competitively, there is a market for massaging horses as well. Who would have figured right?

Therapist familiar with the Game Ready unit, which is a cryotherapy and compression machine used for recovery; has an Equine line that has attachments specifically tailored for horses. Despite being from the country myself, I've yet to ride a horse because I have a slight fear of riding. It is on my bucket-list, but as a result of this fear and the fact the horse cannot communicate their pain parameters, I turned down the offer to add horse massaging to my resume.

Although a smaller market may not have the vast options as a large city, I assure you, you can find a consistent flow for chair events and house calls. If you are within driving distance to a neighboring city, consider even driving there on certain days to market, build your books and to treat clients.

Again, just an example of creating ideas and thinking beyond the norm in building your business.

BACKSTAGE MASSAGE

Getting an opportunity to work backstage for a concert or event can be exciting. If you are like I was in the beginning, you probably have no idea what to expect or how to approach getting booked for this type of gig. I'll give you options on how to get booked and how to prepare for working backstage. First, I'll go over "crashing" a backstage event if you aren't scheduled to work it. Not as invasive as a wedding crasher, but the proper massage crasher technique for a venue.

Backstage Crasher Prep

If you have no connection to work a backstage gig, you can attempt to create a way by showing up at a venue to market your services. For those that want to attempt the following marketing technique, you must be prepared with the following items... DO NOT embarrass yourself or waste crews' time if you don't want to prepare accordingly before showing up.

▶ Have your table in the car and if you have a massage chair, pack that as well because sometimes the work space backstage can be limited.

▶ I also have a small bin or my ZUCA bag packed with towels, Clorox wipes, paper towels, Lysol spray, hand sanitizer, 5 - 8 laminated signs that say MASSAGE, duct-tape, dry-erase marker, at least one set of sheets, business cards and a receipt book.

▶ Pack a few snacks & bottled waters if your backstage crash attempt is successful. Hopefully you will be busy, so if you're thirsty or need something quick to eat to maintain your energy, you have it available.

Most crew, dancers and members of the management do not disrobe entirely, so you can simply use paper towels on head rest for each client, after the table has been cleaned.

You want to have 1 - 2 complete sheet sets handy if you get the opportunity to work on the actual artist as the massage will either be in their dressing room, or their tour bus. In the event the massage takes place on the tour bus, you will just need to bring your massage lubricant, backpack with modality tools you may use and possibly your massage chair if requested. Depending on the bus setup, a table will not likely fit. I personally have not taken my table onto a bus but have used my chair a handful of times.

The Approach

Once you've prepared all your massage items, find the loading dock area by security check-in (usually at the side or back of the venue) and ask to speak with the tour manager; or you can initially knock on one of the busses parked across from the loading dock to pitch your services to a member of the crew first.

You want to show up between 12pm - 3pm usually for an evening show, as the initial madness of stage and backstage setup has been completed, but early enough before doors open at the venue. Also, when showing up early, the likelihood of running into a member of the crew or production is higher because those are high traffic times for setting up.

If they ask who you are, let them know you're a massage therapist and wanted to see if they were in need of a therapist today. If they already have or don't want coverage, ask if they have a few moments so you can introduce yourself and give them a few cards in the event they need your services when they are back in town, and you will give them a free 15 – 20 minute massage for the short inconvenience.

For those nervous about this marketing method, try practicing this at a smaller venue. There's a higher chance they will not have a therapist on hand, unlike a major artist at a larger venue. This shouldn't discourage you from attempting to gain access to work in a larger venue though, because sometimes the therapist on tour may have more than one job title and won't be available to perform or meet all the massage demands for the day. Or the demand for the day could be too great, so they could use an extra set of massage hands.

Just remember that the worst they can say is NO, and don't take it personal if they are short or brash with you whether you are allowed to work or not. There is so much going on backstage before the start of a show and production and crew are juggling several tasks at once.

Make sure to have cards/brochures handy and are the image of the best massage therapist around.

†

I've worked several backstage events but have done one backstage crash at a smaller, but popular, venue. I gave my business pitch stated all the services I offered and noticed some interest, but still sensed a little hesitation. So, I offered being a "runner" as an additional service I provided as well. A runner basically makes food, store, bank and airport runs, and you must keep all receipts and return change for all transactions to be reimbursed.

This crew was needing a store and food run, and the scheduled runner hadn't arrived and was 30 minutes late. So, I gladly accepted the runner position, and when I came back, had people awaiting my massage services. I capitalized on the individual who was late to create an opportunity to showcase my massage skills.

A lesson to not only be prompt and professional, but also to seize the moment when an opportunity arises.

Work Set-Up

If you are allowed back to work, bring your stuff in quickly (make sure your packing system for your tables and supplies is easily mobile), and try to choose a spot near a high traffic area so people know you are there. If security or production tell you to set-up somewhere specific, adhere to their requests.

Once you're set-up, go hang your signs around the backstage area and use your dry erase marker to draw arrows to direct people to the area you are set-up at. During this process try to engage and meet people without invading anyone's personal space, and do not approach headline talent if they pass by you.

When the word gets out that you are there let your talent prevail, and once the show begins, go by production to chat, give the ones available mini massages, and if the moment presents itself, ask to exchange contact info, or at least if you can have their email. Many of the people you meet will potentially be working for another artist or another tour in the future, so leaving the best impression possible can help you getting booked down the line.

Overall you want to blend-in and go with the flow backstage, and its not the environment to be in "fan-mode." So absolutely DO NOT go up to anyone asking for autographs or pictures.

This a sure-fire way to be blacklisted from people in the industry and even a venue.

HOUSE CALLS

Market in areas and in a way that's most comfortable and safe for you. If a situation does not feel right, do not do it. The benefit about running your own mobile massage company is that you are the boss and in control always.

Mobile Massage Apps

For therapist starting out with limited clientele but want to gain as much mobile experience as possible might contemplate signing up for a mobile massage app which is very similar platform to Lyft or Uber but designed for booking a massage therapist for massage. The profit margins will not be as high as your personal bookings, but the experience can assist you in figuring out your scheduling method when booking appointments. It also can help your navigation knowledge when commuting in your area especially during hours you plan on working.

The luxury is you work on clients you didn't have to market for and it can be a safer alternative while feeling out your marketing approach to growing your business. Keep in mind the mobile massage company app will send you a 1099 at the end of the year for your earnings made, so be sure to set a percentage of those earnings aside to cover any fees imposed when filing your tax return.

ENTERTAINMENT VENUES

Most entertainment venues where concerts, sporting events and other shows are held, have their own contract "house vendors" at their disposal. This will include not only massage therapist, but errand runners, physicians and others in the health and wellness field.

You can get in touch with the contact person that coordinates that aspect of the venue and see if you can interview to be added to the list as a house therapist, and even errand runner in the event the scheduled artist or event does not have one traveling with them.

DIVERSIFY HOW YOU MAKE MONEY

You can primarily do house calls, but be open to chair massage events, or even in some cases, considering to be on-call as a therapist for a business or working part-time at a spa to mix-up your environment and have a set schedule for some days. Especially if you haven't built up your massage books enough to solely be able to rely on that income to support you.

You can also sell massage and therapeutic products in person and online that you use in your practice and recommend to clients. You could consider creating your own line of massage products, such as lotions, essential oils and creams to create additional residual income.

Joann Brito

If you have catchy and creative company logo and/or tag lines, you could design and sell company apparel. The options are endless in creating various revenue streams.

PRESENTATION IS KEY

I currently live in Houston, Texas and during the summer months, one can get quite sweaty from traveling and working all day throughout the city, not to mention the traffic one can encounter in between each session; but the overall presentation of how you look, smell and your demeanor are essential components to having a successful massage session for both parties.

PUNCTUALITY

Be prompt as possible when arriving for a session. It's usually ok to arrive 10 - 15 minutes early, but not sooner as the client may not be ready to have you over. If you are going to be early, text your client and let them know you are running ahead of schedule and should arrive at their place within the next 10 to 15 minutes to give them a heads up and so they can wrap up what they are doing and ready once you arrive.

If you anticipate any delay regarding your arrival time for an appointment, communicate it as soon as possible.

I thoroughly communicate with my clients in the event there will be a delay on my arrival if it's going to be more than 10 minutes beyond the time I was scheduled to be at their location.

In the same tone, also hold your clients accountable for not giving you the same communication and respect for your time as you do for them. I have driven through traffic and been in the car over an hour to get to a session, just for the client to not be there or cancel last minute. I give everyone a pass the first time it happens but let them know I understand things come up and I can see an appointment time can slip their mind or unforeseen incidents may happen, but as long as it doesn't happen again, its ok. Now if a client falters and it becomes a repeated occurrence, I do add a fee for the inconvenience, and in some cases, have banned clients from house calls for a period of time.

One year I had so many of my clients not being considerate and taking my time for granted, so during the following season, I chose not to travel anymore on Fridays which is my busiest day during that period and make whoever wants to get worked on come to me. With traffic, gas and frankly just valuing my time, that was the best option for me.

Never feel bad or guilty about making adjustments in your practice as needed.

LOOK

I'll first start out by saying that I'm a huge believer on maintaining a professional but fun and comfortable work environment, and you must be mindful of the energy you project, both visually and physically. Clothes shouldn't be sloppy, ripped, stained or torn. That's why it's important to dress appropriately and give off the vibe you are there for business, nothing more.

It's hard to give off that energy, if say you show up in tight booty shorts, or are wearing clothes that are too revealing. It's not only unprofessional, but if you have a client that's married, has a significant other, etc., he or she may not want you coming over to work on their partner, and ban you from returning. You could have given that client an awesome massage and had no intention of doing anything beyond that, but if your dress attire is too provocative or revealing, this can cause you to lose business based on this perception.

Have a mix of clothing, that range in value. I find good bargains for shirts, tights and pants but may spend more on some tights and pant options periodically as I will wear them more often and I want them to sustain for long periods of time thru work and wash cycles.

There is no need to spend tons of money on clothes but investing in a few good pair of tennis shoes and items you will often wash will pay off in the long run. The enjoyment of this field is that you are not wearing business attire with uncomfortable shoes all day, but you do still want to put effort in your appearance.

SMELL

From breath to body odor I cannot express the importance of the smell sense and how it can have a profound impact on a client's mood and overall emotion during an appointment.

If you're a smoker, a client should never be able to detect you are. Never should any traces of smoke linger on you prior to arriving to an appointment. Travel with a toothbrush and toothpaste, wear a specific shirt or outfit on your smoking breaks and change into a new set of clothing before heading to your next massage.

One may consider to not smoke in their car as the odor can remain on you and your sheets, even if you smoke with the windows rolled down.

If you are "hairy," it may be a good idea to shave, wax or trim down the hair as odor can stay on hair and linger longer.

Body fragrance spray, Summers Eve spray, Gold Bond spray or cleansing post-workout wipes can refresh the skin and remove dirt, oil and odor as a result of sweat and the elements your skin is exposed to throughout your workday.

NAIL MAINTENANCE

Nail beds should be short, clean and neat with no jagged edges as they could cause you to scratch a client. If a client sees you with dirty nail beds, they may be inclined to cancel on the spot. I mean would you want to be worked on for an hour or more from someone you're unsure has even washed their hands for the day? Imagine all the things they could have been doing from eating, massaging whoever else prior to you arriving and even using the restroom without washing their hands. The thought actually makes me quiver a bit... so hands should always be clean and neat.

For those that like to have their nails done, it isn't advised to have long or pointy nails. I personally get an acrylic overlay, and my nails are short and square-shaped. If you do not desire this option, then a simple manicure will do, and your hands will love you for it.

If you are a therapist who likes to work barefoot, please make sure your toes are neatly manicured and have a fresh pedicure. No one wants to look at crusty toes during their massage session. If you are unable to get a pedicure, then have a nice pair of socks on.

Having nice socks is key in general, as some clients will request that you remove your shoes upon arriving inside, so it's always best to be prepared for that when going to a new client.

"For me, luck is preparation meeting the moment of opportunity. There is no luck without you being prepared to handle that moment of opportunity."

Oprah Winfrey

Joann Brito

MASSAGE ESSENTIALS BAG

I'm a back-pack chick and have every size of bag you can think of depending on my work schedule. There are some key essentials I pack, especially during my high-peak work seasons. I'm gone most of the day, so I want to make sure I'm prepared with all my work and personal needs, and you can imagine what I could look and/or smell like if I haven't planned properly for my day.

So, to maintain my energy and presentation at every appointment, these items keep me on track.

†

Make-up bag – With foundation, concealer, blush, and lip gloss. I have the worst racoon eyes, so the natural "fresh-look" doesn't really work for me for that reason, but pack whatever components work best for your skin type.

Also keep in mind not to pile on too much makeup, as it could run and not look pleasant as you sweat.

Body Spray – Perfumes should not be used prior to a session, but a nice floral, vanilla or fresh citrus body spray is always nice in between sessions. I choose this option over traditional perfumes, as they aren't as strong, and I don't want to aggravate a client's allergies if they happen to be allergic or do not like or able to tolerate the smell for an extended period. As stated in the *smell* section, you have other spray and body wipe options

Battery Packs – Being on the go all day, using your cellular device to talk, playing music and GPS can drain your battery on your phone, Bluetooth headphones or credit card processor. I usually have at least 2 different battery packs while commuting, and this is convenient when any of my devices are low on juice.

myCharge is my favorite small battery pack brand because they maintain their charge until you use it and have built in cables and USB ports. I have the myCharge HubMini and HubPlus versions.

Jackery PowerBar is a little bulkier, but it has two USB ports but also has a plug-in adapter to charge a laptop or any device that needs a/c voltage which is a huge plus. I also will use the Jackery to charge my smaller portable chargers when on the go, and it also keeps its charge if you remember to turn it off when you're done using it.

Spare set of clothes – It's important to keep extra clothes in the car in the event of a mishap. I'm clumsy and have spilt drinks and food on myself, and depending on what it is, that smell could linger on you for the day. If there's inclement weather like rain for example and you happen to get drenched, performing a massage is not only uncomfortable, but you also don't want to smell like a wet dog during or after the massage if over.

If you have other sessions planned for the remaining part of the day and are limited with time, having a shirt or another fresh outfit can prevent falling behind schedule if you had to go all the way home to change. I also have clients that smoke, and that odor can stick to your clothes, even if you are not the one smoking so this option is good for those scenarios as well.

Time is money and preventing any setback with time increases your revenue. You would hate for a client to cancel because an incident will cause you to arrive too late and due to the time constraint are unable to receive the massage. I'm also notorious for stepping in water, I have no clue why that is, but it happens at least once a quarter for me, so I always have an extra pair of socks in my car and/or flip flops if this happens.

Hand sanitizer – Every individual should always carry around hand sanitizer because you never know when you need to refresh the cleanliness of your hands, or even an area of a client's body like feet for example. I keep a small sanitizer in my bag and also in one of the pockets of my massage carry case.

Mini Manicure Kit – It will have a nail clipper, tweezers, scissors, nail file. Feel free to add and/or switch out the items with better ones that suit your needs. I replaced the scissors and tweezers in my kit and keep 1 - 2 nail files on hand. You will be so surprised the random times this has come in handy not only for myself, but also for clients while at an appointment.

Gum or Mints – If you choose to use gum, do not chew loud, or pop and blow bubbles. A client shouldn't be able to tell you're chewing gum, and these actions can disrupt a session.

Mints dissolve easier and are another option for those that do not want or like chewing gum.

It's good to choose a flavor type like spearmint or peppermint as it gives off a fresh scent and can last longer.

Snacks – To avoid bad eating habits, which is easy to do commuting most of the day, pack small snacks and even pack a lunch cooler so you can maintain your energy levels throughout the day until you are able to sit for a proper meal.

You may want to invest in a small high-performance insulated lunch cooler, so your lunch can stay fresh and not go bad throughout the day.

Clorox or EPA Wipes – (travel size packs) They are flat and take up less room and much easier to travel with. I use my Clorox or EPA wipes to clean the massage table and any of my massage tools, like my cupping set, Gua Sha tools, etc.

Cooling Agent – Still my favorite is Biofreeze, but I also like a product called Workout Wonder. Both work well with my massage lubricants and clients seems to like it when I use either of these.

Mini Poo-Pourri – Not only is it good to make sure a bathroom space smells good, but one time I ate before a session and it did not settle well in my stomach.

TMI: When I tell you, I blew that bathroom up and could not hold or help it. I did several courtesy flushes, and once I finished put hand soap in the toilet and flushed a few more times to try to decrease the smell as there was no spray in the restroom. I was so embarrassed, but from that point on, I make sure I have body spray or mini poo-pourri in my bag because that is a great smelling fragrance for the toilet. Especially for those death defying BM-sessions and to freshen up any space you are working in by simply spraying into the trash cans in a room.

Cash – I typically do not carry much cash on me, but if I know I'm going to a hotel or anywhere that has valet service, I like to have some cash available to tip the valet attendant or concierge on my way out. On average I tip between $5 - $10 when that situation arises, and tip amount also depends on how helpful they were or if they were nice to keep my vehicle up front.

My clients always joke about how I have everything but the kitchen sink in my backpack, but my philosophy is to be overly prepared when in work mode. It's always good to be prepared with what you need even if you don't use it that day, rather than need a specific item but not have it within reach. You never know when you're going to need one of these tools.

"I've failed over and over and over again in my life. And that is why I succeed."

Michael Jordan

TIPS ON WASHING LINEN

As stated earlier, smell can be an integral component to a massage experience. If a therapist smells, or worse, the sheets don't smell good, it will be a painful hour or more to endure. So not only should your personal scent be important, but the smell of your sheets should be a priority. I once had to end receiving a massage after 25 - 30 minutes because the sheets reeked of cigarette smoke and I couldn't take it any longer. So, I kindly apologized and stated I needed to get up and leave, then left and never saw that therapist again... our first and last encounter.

Clients ask me all the time, "what do you wash the sheets with," or "how do you get your sheets to smell so fresh?" My response, fabric softener. I place a cup and a half of softener in the washer bin with the sheets prior to beginning the cycle and also in the softener dispenser, along with my detergent. Once full wash and drying cycle are complete, the sheets have a long-lasting aroma.

Its normal for your sheets to get slightly stained due to the use of oil or massage lubricants over time. Depending on the fabric of your sheets, small stains barely visible or can be hidden with the top blanket are still ok for use. Severely stained linen should be trashed and replaced with a new set.

An option to see if linen can be salvaged, or if linen has an odor and you want to see if you can remedy it before trashing and buying new ones. You can use Oxy for stain and odor, if sheets are white you can add bleach, as well as adding baking soda to the wash cycle. Attempt this for a few cycles, with detergent, to see if sheets appearance has improved before opting to trash any linen.

Folding Method

When I fold my sheets, I fold the fitted sheet and pillow case and place them on top of one another. Then I fold the flat sheet, but before finishing the last fold of the flat sheet, place the fitted sheet and pillow case in it and fold them all in together. This method is great so when you go to pull sheets needed for appointments, you can simply grab and go as each is a complete folded set.

You're also able to stack them more neatly on your shelves and in your vehicle using this method.

☼ Tip

Get your sheets out of the wash and dryer cycles soon after it completes so they do not smell moldy or musty and do not wrinkle. You can even re-start a dry cycle to fluff them again if they have been sitting in the dryer too long. If you are short on time and not able to fold them all, separate and place them flat across your bed or over a chair until you are able to fold them properly.

Wrinkled sheets have the appearance of not being clean, and clients will wonder if you are reusing a pair of sheets from a previous client. As mentioned earlier, I'm a bit OCD and have even steamed my sheets to get the wrinkles out prior to folding them.

MODALITY OPTIONS

Your hands are the most essential instrument when performing a massage but mixing in additional modalities can enhance and assist in the overall outcome of a session. Keys tips to keep in mind when choosing a modality to add in your mobile practice, try not to choose something that requires an extended amount of time to setup and breakdown.

I used hot stones when I initially started, and although I enjoy the benefits of them, the setup time and time it took for the stones to heat up, in addition to the breakdown time, did not make sense for my mobile practice not to mention pretty heavy to lug around. A client can always choose to purchase a hot stone set for you to use when you come over, but that modality is better for a set massage space, not a mobile practice.

☼ **Tip**

If you still are fixed on offering hot stones in your mobile practice, it would be wise to invest in a Himalayan hot stone set. It is more expensive than your standard stones, but it does not require water to heat the stones up, they heat up faster and can even be used frozen.

I always say if Epsom salt and stones were to create a baby, it would have made Himalayan stones.

Here are some popular modality choices:

Cupping - Cupping is my all-time favorite modality to incorporate during my massage sessions. Primarily because it allows me to manipulate the fascial matrix and tissue in various ways, which allows clients to recover and have improved muscle movement at a faster rate.

I prefer vacuum cupping, but traditional fire cupping is another option.

Gua Sha/Fascia Scrapping Tools - There are so many Gua Sha tools in different shapes, sizes and material on the market. I favor medical grade stainless steel tools because they are more durable and last longer and are more sanitary. Jade is lightweight and more fragile, but very good to use on the face. There are other stone and plastic options if you want a more affordable route, but I wouldn't recommend that choice for long-term use.

Vibrating Massage Device – I used the Theragun for a while and currently use the Hypervolt by Hyperice. Both devices are effective in achieving the goal of stimulating and relaxing the tissue. So, it's simply a preference of which product best suits your needs, but either is a great investment.

Aromatherapy – You can use essential oils to add to your lotion or oil or place a few drops on the headrest or face mask for a massage. Rosemary, Lavender and Eucalyptus are very nice scents to use.

I know therapist who will pack a diffuser, put essential oils in it, and place it under the headrest when the client is face down, and have the aroma cycle thru the entire session. If you do not mind packing this, you can add this to your practice if it benefits you.

You may want to pack a small extension cord to ensure your diffuser can reach under the face cradle if the outlet isn't near the table setup.

Ice Packs – Taking actual ice packs is not ideal, but there are a few options:

I use a cold massage roller ball, it has a removable metal ball which I can take out. I will ask a client if I can use a bowl and ice. I will place the metal ball in the bowl, add ice and then add some water to help the metal ball freeze at a quicker rate. I will do this at the beginning or at least midway thru the session so it's nice and cold when I'm ready to use it on the extremity's that need it.

This option is great because it reminds me when I was a young athlete and use to freeze water in small Dixie cups, and ice an extremity and tear off the paper as it melted. The upside of this product is the mess is limited, and the metal ball stays cold up to 2 hours and has more options of how you ice an area. The fact that the ball has the option to be removed, gives you the ability to clean the entire massage roller thoroughly before and after using it.

So, it's the upgraded version from the Dixie cup I used years ago.

Another option is I will have a client order a gel ice pack that they can keep in their freezer. Or if all else fails, I will make custom icepacks with zip lock bags or use their bathtub to make them a couture cold tub.

Stretching Straps - As stated earlier, I use extremity mobilization straps for assisted stretching with my clients. They resemble seatbelts, and I will use my blanket or a towel to place underneath the strap and client's skin/clothing to make it comfortable once I tighten the straps and to keep that extremity in place while I stretch them. If I don't have a towel packed, I will ask the client is I can use one or two of their towels.

Cooling Agents - There are several cooling agents on the market to aide in decreasing pain and inflammation and increasing circulation and recovery. I get asked often what I use and/or what my favorite products are in this category, and I would have to say Biofreeze & Workout Wonder by Mio are at the top of my list and feel great in my opinion when used with icing. This is not to discredit the several other items on the market, as time to time I do try out and use other products, but those are my favorite.

There are many more modality options offered for sale, some even unique that I haven't listed. One therapist I know uses a product called *Electrons Plus*. Although it's not a product I'm totally accustomed to administering yet, I can see how the effects are beneficial for a client as I enjoyed receiving treatment from it. This is when research and exploring options that will complement your therapy style are important.

You want to be as educated as possible and find and use modality options that enhance your skill set and are ones you are comfortable using. The more services you can offer, will also add to your value as a therapist. Even if certain modality options don't work for you, you may meet other therapist in this discovery process to build networking and business relationships with.

Joann Brito

HOW TO HANDLE...

When people find out what I do for a living, they typically like to ask what's the funniest, weirdest or most uncomfortable session I've encountered. Although some of these memories can be humorous, there are a few situations that can make a session troublesome. The top priority is one's safety, so regardless of the tips and suggestions regarding the situations below, don't feel hesitate about ending a session if you feel your safety is at risk as that's the number one priority.

The second priority is securing the coin, so the following pointers can help you maneuver through each situation to maintain proper boundaries during every massage, while not making a client uncomfortable, (even if you were not the one who initiated the uncomfortable situation), which will cause you not to retain them as a client for future appointments if you desire.

SEXUAL ADVANCES

Let's first talk about the obvious which is if a client makes an advance, either verbally or thru body language at some point during the session. There are a few ways to avoid and get around this situation.

1. I initially play dumb like I don't know or understand what they are expecting in hopes they will just lose the thought or are too fearful to be more forward in their request and will simply relax and go back to enjoying the massage.

2. If that doesn't work, simply state you don't do those type of massages and don't plan on starting now. When saying this, I will say it in a firm, but semi-nonchalant way that doesn't cause them to get too ashamed or agitated.

   An example of comments I've said before: "Boy, I don't do those kinds of massages, haven't you checked my references" ... "I know you don't think I'm giving you a happy ending, you must want your private bits snatched off today, because that's what's going to happen if you ask me again" (The comments may sound a tad joking in nature, but definitely will have someone thinking they could possibly be without their favorite body part if they ask again). Usually comments like these get a laugh and they say they are playing or something to that effect and that's the end of the testing the water phase.

3. For the persistent, and brave, one may make one last ditch effort to see if they can persuade or talk you into giving them some "special attention." At this point, I state my last position of how I cannot assist them with their request, but if they need a minute to go to the bathroom to relieve them self, they can do that quickly, so we can get back to the session because I don't want to keep repeating myself. I then state that if they can't chill out, we can go ahead and end the session.

I have never had any issues after this last step, but never compromise your stance out of pressure or for money... its simply not worth it. I have never had to end a session because of this, as options 1 - 3 typically work, but I have had friends within the industry not as lucky.

In the event you must end a session due to a client continuing to be inappropriate, be sure to document the incident in detail. In your document, include date, time, full details on the incident and location. Most phones have a built-in tracker that has a map of the location you were at and how long you were there. Life360 is another option for location sharing app, and it can also be a way you can share your location with people in your circle that you want to have the ability to track you at every appointment you have scheduled.

Print maps, pictures, texts and any additional documentation to protect yourself. A client could accuse you of sexual misconduct as retaliation for your rejection to give a "happy ending." This is rare, but you can't underestimate someone who continues to violate your boundaries regarding the session.

Keep in mind though, that just because a client "tests" your boundaries and ethics, does not automatically mean they won't be a great long-term client.

☼ Tip

Take the proper steps in properly screening and vetting a new client before scheduling an appointment to go to their home or office. As stated in the *"Safety"* section, Google their name, address, etc. to not only prepare for the session, but also to see if any red flags show up prior to going to a new client you don't know. Implementing a good screening process can keep you safe and give you an added layer of comfort.

Taking a self-defense course can give you added security and boost your confidence in the ability to protect yourself if a situation gets physical.

UNINTENTIONAL AROUSAL

When working on a male client, touch may induce a client to "pitch a tent" as a result of an erection. Although this scenario could happen in the previous situation listed, this action does not necessarily mean that a client's intention, is to engage in inappropriate sexual misconduct.

For those clients not accustomed to being worked on regularly, the psychological feedback the body sends can cause the client to not be in total control of its response to touch.

To keep the client from becoming flustered and uneasy, and in your attempt to remedy the situation:

▶ Move the client into a different position.

▶ If you are familiar with trigger points, you can execute trigger point techniques and massage moves that are effective while also eliciting a bit of a pain response to the neuro-receptors which will assist in diminishing the client's current state. Do not attempt this if you are not fully trained in this approach because you do not want to injure a client, as specific techniques and pressure are being performed in sensitive areas.

▶ Have a thin blanket for every session; you can use this as added draping when necessary to conceal the erection until it subsides.

At no time should you bring attention to the matter, as it could embarrass the client and spoil the experience for the remaining time left in the session. Just keep working and pretend it isn't even there.

CANCELLATIONS

We all know that unexpected situations can occur which may cause a client to cancel an appointment on short notice. When this turns into a regular occurrence, is when it becomes an issue, especially as a mobile therapist. There have been times I've traveled over an hour, in traffic, for a client to cancel when I'm about to arrive to their location; or they simply are not there and have forgotten the appointment all together.

If this is not typical behavior of the client and just a random fluke, I tend to let it slide but stress the inconvenience that situation caused and to better communicate to prevent from this happening again.

If these situations continue to become more frequent, invoke a cancellation policy & fee. As stated in the *Scheduling Software* section, you can use this option to have credit cards stored on file to charge no show or last-minute cancellation fees. Ultimately, have a clear cancellation policy in place and be sure to confirm appointments ahead of time to remind clients of their scheduled session.

DOMESTICS

Verbal Arguments

Being present when a sensitive matter arises, can be an extremely uncomfortable predicament. When an argument ensues, politely excuse yourself from the room, and say you need to go use the restroom or go get something to drink. Do not engage or involve yourself in this verbal dispute.

If kids are in the vicinity, I will see if I can not only remove myself but also them. I'll ask them if they want to come with me to get a snack or ask them to take me to their room to show me their toys. After some time has passed and if the argument seems like it's not coming to a close, I will go gather my things and let the client know we can re-schedule for another day and ask for a partial payment of the service at that time or (if it's a client I see often and have a rapport with) I will add it to the next session.

Some may think this request means you're not empathetic to the situation at hand, but you weren't the cause of the argument and you still spent your time and gas going to the location, so you should be compensated in some way for the inconvenience. I've had clients send or give me gift cards, tickets to a show or game, or will tip more than their typical amount to let me know they feel bad about what transpired.

Many people, including myself, understand when emotions get involved, that a simple discussion or question can unexpectedly turn into World War III; but following it, do not judge or make anyone involved feel embarrassed that it happened in your presence.

For me, a sincere apology is more than enough, and as long as the client takes the necessary precautions so it doesn't happen again, what else can you do but forgive and move on. We've all had at least one "oh shit" moment in our life, right?

Physical Disputes

I have not witnessed first-hand any physical domestic situations between a man and a woman during my career (knocking on wood), but unfortunately have seen friends or family members fight one another on a few occasions. Difficult to watch, but if other friends and family are around, let them handle the situation.

If you are in a position that requires you to intervene to break up a physical altercation, do it safely if you can. If you cannot contain the situation and/or feel you could be potentially injured as well, flee thru the nearest exit with phone and keys in hand if possible. That way you can drive or call for assistance.

If you are unable to grab your phone or keys, find help at a neighbor's house or the closest business. Once you know it's safe, come back to get your things with at least one friend or with authorities present. If the situation goes as far to have authorities there, most likely they are going to ask you for a statement. You can choose to leave one or say no and that you would rather gather your things, so you can promptly leave.

I hope no one must endure a situation like this, but as stated throughout this book, your safety is important, so do what is best for your circumstances.

Hear no evil, see no evil, speak no evil

Say you are performing a massage or even out and about in the city and see a client partaking in some inappropriate behavior, like cheating for example, would you say something to their partner? Everyone may have their own opinion on what should be done, but from personal experience, my answer would be no.

What goes on in a session, whether you agree with what the client is doing or not, should not be divulged. It isn't your place to say anything to anyone, as that's not why you're there or getting paid for. Not to mention it's a violation of a client's privacy to be speaking on what has happened during a massage session.

The same applies outside of a session if I see a client out engaging (whether assumed or not) in inappropriate behavior. Initially I will act as if I don't see them, as to avoid any awkward moment. But if the client comes to speak with me, I say hi and act like everything is fine and as if I saw nothing. It will not benefit you to get involved in anyone's personal matters, because at the end of the day it's no one's business.

It will mess up not only your future earning potential, but your relationship with your client. Also, if a client knows any of your other clients, they can reach out to them and explain what you did and potentially ruin those relationships as well. All the while, the individual you chose to spill the beans to, 90% of the time will ultimately choose to stay with the person you ratted on. So, the option of continuing to build a working relationship will become problematic as your client's trust and bond with you will be broken and they won't want you around.

So frankly speaking, the messenger always gets fucked in the end, so the best option is to steer clear of situations like this. The reality is the problem was there before you saw anything and might continue even after choosing to divulge any information. You must ask yourself, is the chance of putting your business reputation, your livelihood, because this is how you provide for yourself and your family, worth the risk?

Personally for myself, the integrity I have with my client's is what is important to me. I don't feel it's my job to play judge or jury and I would feel much worse being the bearer of news that could potentially break-up a family, a marriage or any relationship. So, my personal choice goes beyond just the financial aspect.

I have clients who have become some of my closest friends go through some major storms in their relationships. I offer my listening ear, understanding and support, and even if I am privy to information unknown to a party, opt to say nothing. But now, we can laugh about the challenges they previously faced and see what beautiful bond and relationship they have grown to have. All while keeping those secrets locked in a box for no one to know.

Every relationship grows in different ways, at different paces and through more "BS" than one would like to admit, but those are your client's journey to go through, and I want to be apart of the good memories, not add to anyone's pain.

Being in this line of work presents its own hurdles as people may "assume" and have preconceived notions about you that could be so far from reality and the truth. Its comical and slightly entertaining the things said about me throughout my career that have been untrue. So, the last thing you need to be worrying about is what is going on in someone else's household… let your craft be the focus.

With friends and family, your thought process can be on the total other end of the spectrum, but in business even though burdensome at times, should not be fully handled from a personal perspective. Your time and energy will be better spent thinking of ways to structure and grow your business.

I feel the only way I would consider getting involved is if someone's personal safety could be in jeopardy (i.e.: worries of suicide, fear of excessive drug use, etc.) as I would not want that on my conscious if the outcome was detrimental.

OPPOSING VIEWS

You are not going to agree or believe in everything your client does, but when it comes to business, attempt to have the premise that the client is always right.

Don't engage much by expressing your true feelings on topics that could become heated and cause a client to judge you, which in evidently could lead to you not getting future business.

Top 2 topic conversations to shy away from:

▶ Religion

▶ Politics

These topics could be a never-ending debate and difficult to avoid, but it has the potential to get awkward and uncomfortable if you have varying views. Ultimately your viewpoints have no influence on how well you perform your job, so it's not wise to have your inclination overshadow your craft.

Simply change the subject to another topic or if you initially thought you could have a sensitive topic conversation with a client but see the conversation is going in a total direction unexpected, you can simply state that you're always interested in different points of view and perspective on issues even if they are not fully in line with yours. Then ask what their plans are for the weekend, or if they heard about a concert or movie playing worth seeing... anything to change the subject smoothly to the next discussion.

CONFIDENTIALITY AND DISCRETION

Confidentiality and discretion are important, especially for sensitive situations like some of the examples listed, but you will build client trust and retention when these are kept private. If you work on high profile clientele, businessmen and even certain events, don't be surprised if you are required to sign a non-disclosure agreement (NDA), prior to beginning the job to protect the client's privacy.

Don't take offense to this request, and if the terms listed in the NDA are within limits you can abide by, go ahead and sign it as it's only a formality to allow a client to feel comfortable with you working for them. If there is something you do not understand or have questions regarding the contract, feel free to ask or voice your concerns if you have them.

When clients know your expectations and you thoroughly communicate upfront and in a professional and constructive way, you can eliminate and/or handle each of these situations with ease.

"Success is doing what you want to do, when you want, where you want, with whom you want, as much as you want."

Tony Robbins

SELF-CARE

As a therapist, sometimes the biggest problem is finding and setting the time aside to take care of ourselves. If you want to have a long career and be able to sustain a steady workload, selfcare is necessary.

So, we will have to take the same advice we give our clients, and do some of the following:

▶ *Pamper Yourself* - Get massages, facials, have regular mani and pedi's, and added body treatments if available.

▶ *Stay Hydrated* – Sufficient hydration keeps you functioning properly for the day, but also helps maintain the suppleness of your skin.

▶ *Adequate Nutrition* – With a mobile practice, if you don't plan out your meals and set aside time to eat, you'll most likely find an unhealthy option on the go. Having filling but light meals like smoothies, fruit, salads or sushi for example, won't leave you feeling heavy or lethargic like pastas or carbs.

▶ *Workout* – Go for a run or join a yoga, pilates or spin class or any exercise you enjoy doing. The activity can clear your mind and build your overall stamina for massage sessions.

▶ *Body Recovery* – The benefits of a sauna, having ice baths, acupuncture, IV drip therapy, stretching and cupping, can lengthen the career of a massage therapist.

▶ *Meditate & Reset* – Even if it's only for 10 – 20 minutes at a time, taking moments to breath and refocus can be a marvelous tool for your well-being. You don't realize how much energy, both good and bad, is transferred between you and the client's you work on.

I've had days where I've only worked on 2 clients that left me completely drained, as if I worked on 6 clients for the day. Meditation helps re-center your mind, regain energy and overall boosts your mood and happiness level.

I've had therapist begin yoga sessions to help them not only exercise and improve their own flexibility level, but also train and assist in the process of practicing meditation.

▶ *Rest & Relaxation* - Sometimes you need to take time for yourself and simply shut-off from the world. Set aside a day to sleep in, spend time with friends and family, have a long workout session, hang out by a beach or plan a quick getaway.

If time constraints don't allow for me to take a vacation, or if I want to save money but still have the experience of being away, then I will plan a stay-cation. I'll book a room at a hotel, lounge by the pool, book spa treatments if the hotel has one and even plan a night out in the city or just hang out in the hotel bar area.

My friends ask, why not just stay at home? When I'm home I think of things I need to be doing while I'm there and don't fully relax. It's nice to know housekeeping will clean the room and a simple call to room service will bring me breakfast or dinner in bed. Also networking at the hotel with other guests, concierge and staff becomes easier as they get to know you and feel more comfortable referring business.

Your hands and body are the driving force of your massage business, so if that breaks down, the foundation of your practice will be affected. Throughout your life and career, continue to work on your consciousness to stay grounded and centered. This will help fuel your connection with everyone you encounter, especially for those that are receiving a treatment from you. Remember, self-care is the best care and you don't need to apologize or get permission for putting yourself first from time to time!

"Rest and self-care are so important. When you take time to replenish your spirit, it allows you to serve others from the overflow. You cannot serve from an empty vessel."

Eleanor Brown

INVEST IN YOUR CRAFT

NEVER STOP LEARNING

I've been in this business a little over 10 years now and I still get a thrill learning new techniques and incorporating a different modality to enhance my sessions. I spend hours reading and researching information, on massage, the health and wellness field, meditation, and in business. Purchase books and utilize all the resources the internet has available.

In addition to researching, keep your skill set up by taking hands-on classes. The web has given everyone the ability to access virtually anything from your phone or computer, which overall is very beneficial, especially with individuals with limited funds, but the desire to physically attend courses has decreased because of the convenience of online content.

Although this option is a bonus, it lacks the ability to give your artistry a more accurate approach for the delivery and the execution of specific techniques. This is a "touch" based field and the internet can only teach and go so far, so don't lose the benefit of what hand-on courses can provide.

PRACTICE, PRACTICE, PRACTICE

Practice new techniques on friends and family and get feedback. It's good to see what they like and don't like, and it usually isn't hard to find a friend or family member that doesn't want free body work in exchange for some honest and constructive critics.

I'm consistently asked what reading material and hands-on courses I suggest to enhancing a massage therapist skill-set. The following are people and items I've purchased and researched to further add to my knowledge of the human body. Once you become familiar and can grasp the methodology regarding the fascial structure, movement and response, it will give you a better understanding on my next book explaining my approach on how I treat a client.

I have not had the opportunity to take any hands-on courses yet with these companies', but their written and web content is pretty fascinating, and has given me the necessary insight to achieve optimal results for my clients and guide me in tailoring my own personal treatment method.

▶ Tom Myers, the creator of *Anatomy Trains*, has had over 40 years of wisdom and experience in fascial therapy and research. His products offer the most detailed description of the fascial matrix and structural integration and when coupled with movement and touch can manipulate, treat and heal the human body.

This is the short but simple description, which does not do his total work justice, as you will not find content regarding this topic as thorough as he has done it.

I have purchased a handful of his books; webinars and I believe I have viewed almost every bit of content accessible online.

▶ Ann and Chris Frederick, founders of *Stretch to Win* and creators of *Fascial Stretch Therapy*, designed a neuromyofascial system to merge assisted stretching and fascia movement.

Their manual therapy and movement re-education are unique and gives an additional outlook on not only increasing a client's level of flexibility, but also understanding, correcting and strengthening a client's imbalances.

▶*Animal Flow* is a ground-based movement workout using your bodyweight. I'm having fun exploring this new method since I feel its important to find unique and varying ways to move your body because it helps mobility, strength and additionally is a way to keep your fascial structure restored and hydrated.

†

These resources are at the top of my list for gaining fundamental knowledge on the human anatomy, and to have as references when I want a refresher on a specific topic. They are also the elite hands-on courses I look forward to attending in the future, as I believe the in-person instruction will surpass what I've learned in any of the written or web contents I've read and seen thus far.

Bottom-line, you will not regret investing in these companies' books, workshops, products and webinar content available.

PASSION

Massage is an art form and you must love bodywork and the human body to get into this business. If you are easily repulsed or disgusted by a physique that's not perfect, or a bit of a prude in your approach to working on the body, then massage may be a difficult profession to pursue. Additionally, don't get into this occupation because you want to meet someone famous, or with ill intentions or an unrealistic view of what will be required to become great in this field. In saying that, some of you may only be able to do this on a part-time basis as this line of work requires a lot of physical effort and can be taxing on your body, and that's okay too.

The business can offer many perks and one can make a great living with a massage career, but it is very hard work. Performing your craft with a smile while exuding good energy, even on a day you aren't in a massaging mood will be required from time to time. Which can be said with pretty much any occupation right?

There are also going to be days you want to strangle your client's, or the traffic and commuting is so stressful you want to quit all together, but as you see how your work is benefiting your clients, it is without a doubt an accomplishing and rewarding feeling. The fact that clients book you to alleviate their pain, give them relief from the stresses of life and promote their overall well-being, gives you an edge because they look forward to seeing you.

If bodywork and massage are your passion stay steady on your course of learning, growing and being present and patient through your process. Having the talent is only half the battle but having good business practices, morals and work ethic are character traits that will always pay off in the end.

†

This book is simply a blueprint of ideas and recommendations as a starting point to build your mobile massage business. Some will stay with you throughout your career and many will fluctuate with time as new business and therapy products, as well as massage techniques are introduced to the market. Don't rush, but ease into the business at the pace you're comfortable with.

If you try something and it doesn't work, or mistakes are made throughout your growing process, don't get discouraged. Every client, every experience and even your missteps are all a part of the journey, so expand on these ideas and create something magical.

As you test out some of these suggestions, please feel free to share your progress and experiences with me. I would love to hear all feedback, and I wish everyone well on their mobile massage business endeavors.

Love You Mean it! ♥

"If you can't figure out your purpose, figure out your passion. For your passion will lead you right into your purpose."

TD Jakes

NOTES

www.ingramcontent.com/pod-product-compliance
Lightning Source LLC
Chambersburg PA
CBHW052053070526
44584CB00017B/2162